celestial navigation

poems by

Peter Vanderberg

Finishing Line Press
Georgetown, Kentucky

celestial navigation

Copyright © 2021 by Peter Vanderberg
ISBN 978-1-64662-510-9 First Edition
All rights reserved under International and Pan-American Copyright Conventions. No part of this book may be reproduced in any manner whatsoever without written permission from the publisher, except in the case of brief quotations embodied in critical articles and reviews.

ACKNOWLEDGMENTS

"Son of Waves,"—*Prairie Schooner*
"Drownproof," "First Night at War," "Forenoon Watch,"—*Action, Spectacle*
"Dhow Close Astern,"—*O-Dark-Thirty*
"Sea Heaps Up,"—*Drunken Boat*
"Mass Casualty Drill,"—*Unbroken Journal*
"Celestial Navigation,"—*The Harpoon Review*
"Near Gale,"—*Manhattanville Review*
"Lost at Sea,"—*War Literature & the Arts: An International Journal of the Humanities*
"Scattered White Horses,"—*CURA: A Literary Magazine of Art and Action*

Publisher: Leah Huete de Maines
Editor: Christen Kincaid
Cover Art: James Vanderberg
Author Photo: Elizabeth Vanderberg
Cover Design: Elizabeth Maines McCleavy

Printed in the USA on acid-free paper.
Order online: www.finishinglinepress.com
also available on amazon.com

Author inquiries and mail orders:
Finishing Line Press
P. O. Box 1626
Georgetown, Kentucky 40324
U. S. A.

Table of Contents

Son of Waves 1

Seascapes 2

Near Gale 4

First Night at War 5

Gentle Breeze 6

Sea Heaps Up 7

Man Overboard! 8

Violent Storm 9

Drownproof 10

Mass Casualty Drill 12

Forenoon Watch 13

Dhow Close Astern 14

Gale 15

Celestial Navigation 16

Scattered White Horses 17

Lost at Sea 18

The Watch Officer's Guide to TAO 19

Reading Leaves 22

Calm 23

Psalm for the Last Day of Summer 24

Notes 25

For Liz

*Who has measured the ocean
in the hollow of his hand,
or with the breadth of his hand
marked off the heavens?*
—*Isaiah 40:12*

Son of Waves

> *He hushed the storm to a gentle breeze,*
> *& the billows of the sea were stilled.*
> —Psalm 107

You are healthy,
growing faster than we thought,

you always will be.   Bones

flash in ultrasound
                    bright silver   & fleeting.

You moved.   *A boy.*
           Your mouth was open   (a boy).

arc of skull   ribcage   spine

       Your name means *tide flow*   means
       born near the sea   son of waves.

    Be born soon.

                        The wars are not going well

& people everywhere begin to despair.

Seascapes

HMS Woolwich
13 January, 1806

Commander Beaufort begins his journal,

Hereafter I shall estimate the force of wind according to the following scale

        0.   calm
        1.   light air
        2.   light breeze
        3.   gentle breeze
        4.   moderate breeze
        5.   fresh breeze
        6.   strong breeze
        7.   near gale
        8.   gale
        9.   strong gale
      10.   storm
      11.   violent storm
      12.   hurricane

Beaufort gauged what each wind would allow:
    light air: *bare steerageway with all sails set clean & full*
Lookouts watch seascapes—
        from lifelines   to horizon
        watch—
            small wavelets   *glassy crests unbroken*
        watch—
            scattered   *white* *horses*
            name this wind   *gentle breeze*
  another
            gale

Sailors know   *when sea heaps up*
            & white foam   *streaks off breakers*
at home   *whole trees are moving—*
    if she is out walking
          her hair blows   wild
    & the wind resists her leaving.

            ———————

Naming the invisible   by how it moves
          the visible
knowing seen & unseen—
       the lookout feels   breeze-borne gale

forecasts   *storm*
         & another ship will return from sea.

Near Gale

Between imagination & truth   memory grew fingers
    in my mother's womb as she wrote
her thesis paper: "Ripples of Surrender—
Japanese Literature After World War II."

      Every cup of tea became ceremony.

Mother-writer   thinking over horizons
    of psyche   took sides with a people
her father was sent to kill.
She shared   their death-resistance
against the conquest   of American men.

    Her first child was birthed under threat of the knife.

Asian Studies called   from high bookshelves
    over games of war & backyard adventure.
Tall enough to reach   I found Bushido   & mountains
    of recluse poems
        scratched   on trees & temple walls.

    Strange prophesy—water-bound son,
reading haiku   off the coast of Pakistan
    standing watch so his ship doesn't   drag anchor
or loosen the grip of deterrence.   I am the gray warship
      between their children   & the winded sea.

    I am insignificant.
                  I am writing to apologize.

First Night at War

> *Underestimating your enemy means thinking he is evil.*
> *Thus you destroy your three treasures*
> *& become an enemy yourself.*
> —Lao-tzu

Off the coast of war General Quarters woke the hive. Helmets & flack jackets donned on the run toward deck guns. I heave open a watertight door: Horizon flash—no thunder. Another. Between mute bursts I face Afghanistan & remember the Pashtun. Unwritten nomadic laws demand revenge & asylum.

My ghost sits with tribal elders drinking chai, translating the word *enemy*.

Or I am the enemy sending bullets to hearts & minds.

Or I am safe at sea squaring my fear of death with those deaths silently brightening my horizon.

Gentle Breeze

scattered white horses

leaves & small branches
in motion

I taught my children
a game called *war*

Sea Heaps Up

Sara wants me to read her book. I want to watch the news. We try both. Between pages of Little Bear & Mama Bear making cakes, the story of a soldier home from war. After nights & days of screaming his daughter would pull away & say, *You're not my daddy.* He saw the dead in waking dreams walking with his daughter lying on the couch, wordless mouths opening & closing.

Sara presses her hand to my head & pushes back to the page saying, *read daddy, read book.*

"So Little Bear went all by himself—all by himself in new snow."

He went for help at the VA hospital but deployment rumors leaked & he locked himself in a room with Death.

After the news Sara molds my face like play-doh until she forms one she knows.

Man Overboard!

No one noticed the sailor swallow horizon before he jumped. No one heard his laments over seahawk rotors & engine roar. He leapt like a cigarette butt flicked into wind. From the flight deck ocean snaps bone, erases mind—but it will hold you up to say good-bye to air & sun. What longing for home? What solitude on a ship of three-thousand souls sent him over the side?

The penalty for despair is Captain's Mast—*Endangering lives other than your own.* Master-at Arms will take him to a seahawk, bound for the brig back home.

Home   is the new   exile.

Violent Storm

foam patches
cover the sea

visibility
almost lost

kyrie eleison

Drownproof

    [lauds]

Stay optimistic. Our time adrift is likely to be brief & relatively comfortable. Tell motivational stories: There once was a fisherman lost at sea. He collected rain water, ate fish. Four months later he walked ashore, drownproof.

    [prime]

The life raft is equipped with everything we need: first-aid kit, compass, pocket knife, signal mirror, blankets. Learn survival before disaster. Train for the unimaginable.

    [terce]

Without water, delirium comes within four days, death in ten. Drink rain. Do not drink urine. Do not drink seawater.

    [sext]

Tear cloth & weave into fishing line. A hook can be made from a safety pin. Ocean fish can be eaten raw. However, avoid poisonous:
    trunkfish

                                                pufferfish

                    toadfish

stonefish

                          parrotfish

                                              triggerfish

             cowfish

        boxfish

                        filefish

                                          lumpfish.

Sea birds may land on our raft. Kill & eat immediately. Feathers can be used to insulate clothing, bones make fish hooks, beaks make lures. The downy breast can be made into a hat.

[nones]

Don't trail hands or feet in water if sharks are present. If we can kill a shark, they are good to eat. However, the blood of a shark will attract other sharks. Screaming underwater may put off an approaching shark.

[vespers]

After a time adrift at sea, one may stand still & weep. One may dive off the raft to "go below for a cup of coffee." Make short term personal goals. Maintain faith in America by singing patriotic songs.

[compline]

Never press spiritual considerations if doing so divides the group or creates dissension. Exercise personal religious rituals, if any. Practice silent meditation.

[matins]

If no life raft is available, "play dead" to stay alive at sea. Face down, arms & legs loose—relax. Lift your head to breathe & scan horizon for birds, boats, flotsam. Do not waste energy screaming (unless sharks are present). In this way you can drift for days—drownproof.

Mass Casualty Drill

Bodies lined on the flight deck warm in the sun, joke & fake death. Clear skies, light breeze: perfect day for a Mass Casualty Drill. Doc leads his new guy over to practice CPR. The dead man shouts, *He's not gonna kiss me is he?*

On the bridge they wear helmets & hesitate over laminated procedures. Fill berthing spaces with black smoke, sea water, limbless mannequins. It's my turn to reach for the captain with a fake wound in my face & mouth the words, *Help, it's not bad but I need to go home.* He'll pretend to pretend I'm o.k. as I'm carried to the flight deck & lain beside a dead sailor tangled in nightmare: *this is not a drill.*

Forenoon Watch

Engine Room rounds—I find Machinist Mate Bruce
wavering behind the boiler, staring down a gauge.
His eyes, dull like a sick animal's, are slow
to distinguish me from machinery or memory.
I ask how his big date was.

Sir, (he laughs) *she tasted like peach cobbler.*

Not peaches, but cobbler: that home sweetness,
ripe fruit, softened, wet, broken crust.

Bruce leads me to the devil's chair.
Between bulkhead & furnace, one needle trembles
just below catastrophe. Iron heat evaporates thought.

Look sir, my damn kneecaps sweat through my pants.

The pitch of Bruce's laughter rises to fever,
then drowns in the groan of turbines.

Dhow Close Astern

Through the Straits of Hormuz dhow boats swarm. Fishermen & merchant smugglers worked these waters for thousands of years before we stood watch on warships—arms crossed, scowling down at the traffic of dhows. Any wooden boat painted bright yellow & green, crewed by sons, could be full of a death triggered by prayers.

We enter Arabian waters as if we own them. As if the dhow captains read our Notice to Mariners: *Stay clear 500 yards*, or risk force from pencil flare to live fire in a last heartbeat.

Every boat crosses our bow too close. Lookouts warn: *Dhow, close astern!* Our sentinels grip deck guns wired tight to rip tracer rounds through any (credible) threat. I suspect every dhow captain wants us dead. I suspect every one of my gunners wants to sink a dhow.

Gale

crests break into spindrift

twigs break off trees
walking made difficult

the wind warns
return   *return*

Celestial Navigation

> *for Liz*

The ship's deck slowly rises & settles
on the night sea. I study celestial charts,
track a satellite's red-pulse through binoculars.
As the moon ripens over the black horizon
I bend memories with Mercator lines past home
& all the girls who lingered far enough away,
orbiting at a safe distance.
The woman in the moon is full now,

mouth slightly opened in a half-smile, half-
gasp surprise. She blushes with another's sunset.
I settle between swells on the memory
of her who eclipses ship, sea, stars—
> Whispering into the ocean's ear
> I wait for her salty-sweet breath.

Scattered White Horses

What is strange is not the stories my grandfather told
or that I believed I too could be a man.
His finger was bent at forty-five degrees & I had recently
been given my first pocket knife: both proof of mythology.

What is strange is not that I grew up on the brushed-up
waters of the Great South Bay under the out-to-sea
gaze of a father who was his best at the ocean gathering
driftwood furnishings, sending his sons over waves back to shore.

What is strange is not that I joined the navy out of fear
of becoming an ordinary man, as if making decisions
out of fear isn't ordinary. As if choosing myth
over the daily compositions of life isn't ordinary.

The strange thing is that mythology requires such few proofs:
seagulls crying over my father's house,
my grandfather's bent finger, a knife in my pocket—
& that these made the other side of the world less strange to me.

Lost at Sea

bridge-wing lookout—

      calculating what time it is
      back home
      what season of trees.

I stare down to the bow wake   frothing

      phosphorescent algae
& remember

sitting in church   lost

      in the homily

staring at electric prayer candles

        tiered below St. Anthony's feet.

    Both lights reveal the dark

god

in whom I drown.

The Watch Officer's Guide to TAO

I drift like a wave on the ocean,
I blow as aimless as the wind.
    —Lao-tzu

        Nowhere   is there a parallel
in the hands of
              every moment
        TAO is especially important because
                      the watch
   belongs to
        TAO

              Open yourself to the TAO,
           then trust your natural responses
           & everything will fall into place.

       the officer at sea
is required to keep
        TAO
to make sure that he understands clearly
        If   there will be fog
        If   he is wise

            Can you step back from your own mind
                and thus understand all things?

   vision, both outside & inside
       must extend beyond

         his watch

a sense of proportion
    when
        every instant   darkened
the calm   of a Sunday afternoon   at anchor

>   *Darkness within darkness.*
>   *The gateway to all understanding.*

                        time at sea

will awaken

                special talents

           things begin to sort themselves out

>   *Prevent trouble before it arises.*
>   *Put things in order before they exist.*

human understanding
      might not be readily available when wanted.
the essential
                  TAO

               should be studied carefully

As an old salt said: "Relieve in haste, repent at leisure."

>   *Rushing into action, you fail.*
>   *Trying to grasp things, you lose them.*

      Things to be avoided:
      1.   clumsy or redundant language
      2.   emergencies
      3.   word that is not of concern
      4.   church   except in emergencies
      5.   a long list
      6.   use of the phrase "now bear a hand"
      7.   demands
      8.   Pauses, hesitations, & breaks   written down

on watch

        there are many occasions
            when a touch of humor is
                disaster

                coax your mind from its wandering
                & keep to the original oneness

      Erasures
  bring   validity
        into question

                The Master observes the world
                    but trusts inner vision.

All vision depends on
      a slow roving gaze

                Do you have the patience to wait
            till your mud settles & the water is clear?

It is the proper way to begin.

Reading Leaves

Chance is buried under hope & weather.
Storm pushes one ship home calls another away.

On Seaview Avenue they call Mrs. Shandel
when the moon promises birth, marriage or death.

A mother arrives at my door, asks me her life.
She wants me to read for her Johnny overseas.
What would you have me tell her?

Tea swallowed, the seer instructs:
swirl the leaves & turn the cup over.

Fortunes cling to the rim.
Her face clings to her child.

Our men don't return anymore.

Wind shift, storm clouds—the leaves
promised we would come home.

Calm

sea like a mirror

—no wind—

mirror like a sea

Psalm for the Last Day of Summer

Among mussel encrusted breakers
revealed by dead-low tide,
plovers scavenge the day's sacrifice.

In the shallows between beach & sea,
my children tumble in the surf, surprised
by sand giving way beneath their feet.

We come at this late hour to face ocean
& burn once more, speaking scattered tongues
which even our beloved misunderstand.

It was a good day. Tomorrow we may
incite another war. We may need to draw
upon the slow burn & plover's call

when the tide brings our children (God
forbid) something other than laughter.

Notes

"Seascapes," and the wind poems (centered), draw language and inspiration from the Beaufort Wind Scale, which estimates the force of wind based on its visible effect at sea and on land. The scale is still in use today.

"Drownproof" draws upon various sources of US Navy guides for survival at sea, primarily the 1964 Special Issue: Safety and Survival At Sea, *All Hands Magazine*.

"The Watch Officer's Guide to TAO" is a found poem from *Watch Officer's Guide*, eleventh edition, Naval Institute Press, 1979. The italicized, right aligned portions are selections from the *Tao te Ching*, translation by Stephen Mitchell. In the U.S. Navy, the Tactical Action Officer (TAO) is in tactical control of the ship, especially in regards to threat-analysis and reaction. TAO also refers to the essential principle / way of Taoism.

Peter Vanderberg is the author of *Weather-Eye* (Ghostbird Press), and *Crossing Pleasant Lake* (Red Bird Press). His poems have appeared in journals such as *Prairie Schooner, Drunken Boat, Lumina, Cura,* and *Modern Haiku*. He is the Founding Editor of Ghostbird Press, publishing chapbooks that incorporate both writing and visual art.

After serving in the U.S. Navy from 1999–2003, he received an MFA in Creative Writing from Queens College, City University of New York. Peter teaches English and writing at Chaminade High School and is currently pursuing a Ph.D in English at St. John's University, NY. He lives on Long Island with his wife and four children.

www.ingramcontent.com/pod-product-compliance
Lightning Source LLC
LaVergne TN
LVHW041518070426
835507LV00012B/1665